WE INHERIT WHAT THE FIRES LEFT

POEMS

WILLIAM EVANS

SIMON & SCHUSTER PAPERBACKS

NEW YORK LONDON TORONTO SYDNEY NEW DELHI

Simon & Schuster Paperbacks
An Imprint of Simon & Schuster, Inc.
1230 Avenue of the Americas
New York, NY 10020

First Simon & Schuster trade paperback edition March 2020

SIMON & SCHUSTER PAPERBACKS and colophon are registered trademarks of Simon & Schuster, Inc.

For information about special discounts for bulk purchases, please contact
Simon & Schuster Special Sales at 1-866-506-1949 or business@simonandschuster.com.

The Simon & Schuster Speakers Bureau can bring authors to your live event.
For more information or to book an event contact the
Simon & Schuster Speakers Bureau at 1-866-248-3049
or visit our website at www.simonspeakers.com.

Interior design by Ruth Lee-Mui

Manufactured in the United States of America

1 3 5 7 9 10 8 6 4 2

Library of Congress Cataloging-in-Publication Data is available.

ISBN 978-1-9821-2739-8
ISBN 978-1-9821-2743-5 (ebook)

Dedicated to Beverly and Linda and Langston and William.
Who sacrificed so much to make their granddaughter possible.

CONTENTS

Storytelling is a form of tribal propaganda
—Will Storr

GRASS GROWING WILD
BENEATH US

THE ENGINE

The sun fell out of the window,
our daughter caught it with her teeth.

Every nightfall
is a black they can't murder.

The days my car makes it
to the garage are the days I can live forever.

Even flattened against the street, an officer's
knee in my back, I look young for my age.

They say you can chart time by stargazing or
knowing all the stars you see are already dead.

If the tops of trees are the newest life, everything
from my father's land looks like the future.

When I retrieve the mail, I am reminded
of what can outlive me.

When I was a boy, we gathered
sticks that resembled bones.

We tried to resurrect our ancestors, but they refused.
We have given you death once, why would you give

that back?

I had a cut above my eye once
and assumed everything I saw was bleeding.

The ground is better at giving us names
than the sky has ever been.

THE TRAIL SAYS THREE POINT ONE MILES

We know how old we are by remembering
our company while   we walked this trail
      the beginning when there were less
of us   jogging and counting the miles

sweaty and owning our breath   we drove
to your condo which was still our   home
      and showered for a long spell
picking the   wild from each other   then

when we were   pregnant and you refused
to not finish the trail   I was so cautious then
you   would probably never succumb to anything
but I was   brutish and remembered

            this wasn't your first pregnancy
      only the one that had lasted   this long

later   we brought the stroller because
      she loved the buzzing air too   sometimes

she would run along with you like a second hand
      catching up to the hour   sometimes
she stayed in the stroller   . while I pushed
her up each hill   once we saw   a deer

      slowly venturing through the thick
head high as a lighthouse   the brush parting
like a royal court   the girl sat upon
      my shoulders saying   daddy daddy

daddy   until the other deer   emerged
       and there was nothing left
to say   we had been here before   all
of us   with the grass growing wild
       beneath us

INTERROGATION

The morning has rhythm—
wake her up, get dressed, eat
breakfast, brush teeth,
shoes on, then the door. It is
true, even if it is still a sprint.
Not every morning is made from
God, so it is left to me to improvise
upon the machine. Bring
the clothes downstairs, eat in the car
or be ready to pack everything
you can. She is fully dressed,
hoping the morning
will make me forget that she
needs to brush her teeth. It does
not. *I can't brush my teeth if
I already have my shoes on.*
She knows this is not
how logic moves around us,
and yet she tries. Not all
gulfs will be this easy to bridge.
She calls the baseball a football
and I correct her. She says
her grandparents are in heaven
now and I say close enough. I never
know what windows are worth
destroying. She knows that I am Santa.
I have driven into the night and returned
with ice cream at her request then
betrayed her by smiling about it. Lost
a game of Connect Four twice. Pretended
to not see her hiding behind the couch.
Told her why she will never have
a brother. Once we roamed around

the woods and watched a deer
beautiful and liquid move among
the tall grass. The girl's eyes widened
until light came from them. She whispered
even though the deer knew we were
there. *Daddy, it's so cool,* she would say.
And I was silent. Smiling, I thought,
Did you know some people shoot them?

SOFT PRAYER FOR THE TEETHING

Be it the miracle wounding.
Be it the tearing of one's own
body to allow invasion. Be it
the song that won't be suppressed.
The courtship that only happens
at nightfall. The flattering
that happens from outside
the window, but must shatter
the window to be heard. Be it
the ceremony of ache, the feigned
consent. The world opening
inside of a mouth. May these gods
enter and never leave. May they
never be betrayed by a car crash
or unloved lover. May the pain be
a gate broken once and mended again
and again and

LITTLE LIE

Close to her school the lights of the ambulance
splay across the interior of the car. I see

the new shades of my daughter recycle
across her opened face. There is a car in front

of the ambulance, nothing we can see wrong
with it except for the not moving. It is angled in

the turning lane like an invasive sunray into a quiet
room, a thorn among stalks. The bicycle lies

much farther away, the front wheel contorted
around the wooden pole emerging from the concrete.

The back wheel is gone, as if slid in some
mischief's pocket. Chain loose and resting

on the sidewalk. There are no people among
the macabre, unless you count the ghosts. My daughter

asks what happened and I lie the little lie.
I don't know what happened, love.

I say it again and again like a chant
or a wish or something to fill the air

until the lights light up someone else's sky
and can do nothing more than chase us.

MIMIC

Copycat: Mimic:
    the little girl knows this game
now, repeating everything said in front
of her, bubble, giggle between
each failed   attempt. Tortured
her friends all day and now starts
    in on her mother.
Put your shoes away
    your shoes away.
What do you want to
    what do you want
eat
    eat.

When she begins to place
my words in her mouth
    the jump is not far for her—
she is already my mimic after all,
having taken my nose
and eyes and smile for her   own.

Ok: Ok:
    Stop: Stop   Now: Now

My words are the least of her talent,
    though she looks like me in absolute
silence, arms tied like a bow across
    the whole of me/her until I solve
the riddle with silliness as I begin
tickling her   until she can't take
it, thrashing   on our floor

Daddy: Daddy
    Stop: Stop   Not: Not
        Fair: Fair
You're: You're   Cheating: Cheating

I don't apologize for breaking the rules
between my fingers   as I've broken
things not as easily forgivable between
them before   and it's this I want
    to blanket before my mimic picks
up on it, before she takes away another part
    I'm not ready to laugh away.

BECAUSE I WAS ONCE GOOD

I know how difficult baseball is and because she is
good at most things, I know how my daughter reacts

when she fails at something. It's baseball today,
yesterday was archery with a plastic weapon,

and every day is handstand day. The red bat slung
across her shoulder like she has been here before,

I warn how hard it is to hit a ball moving
at you, I try to prepare the ground beneath her

new gravity, admittedly more for my sake
than hers. She hits the first ball, then the second,

only missing on my too-low toss, every contact
brings a levitation of triumph: *I hit it again, Daddy.*

I too am caught in this firework, the uncanny
learning of ascension, and ask, *Do you want to play*

softball, love? and she says, *Um, not really,*
as she connects again, the ball sailing out of view.

ON THE FIRST SNOWFALL

my daughter begged me to play outside
so we wrapped ourselves in every shield
we could find. I try to tell her about the frostbite

that took her great-grandfather's fingers and made
him left-handed, but she never met him, so she
looks at me like, *Whatever.* In the snow for twenty

minutes, which might as well be generations, and
when I tell her we've lost enough heat to never truly
be the same, she dunks her face into the only

untrampled patch of yard we have left and comes up
for air, a fallen night's worth of frost on her face.
Doesn't my beard make me older? Of course

she doesn't look older, but she does look less mine
than she did a moment ago and since this is what
getting older means, I say, *Yes, love,* before

I disappoint her or she disappears into the wind or
until the snow lingers so long, I can no longer tell
the seasons by what collects beneath us.

INHERITANCE

Every year we freeze
our asses off to buy

a fresh Christmas
tree. My wife asks

patiently why we
continue this practice:

a metal tree makes
more sense, probably

better for the earth,
probably better on

our backs, budget,
but my pops always

wanted fresh trees
even when he didn't

have a family to gather
around it, even when

Christmas became
another cold day

interrupting the week.
If I'm honest, I don't know

what idols to keep
and what blood oaths

to break—I don't love
anything enough

to forget its birth.
I don't hold any sin

separate from
the father. I take

all the history
into my mouth

and swallow
without tasting.

I pull a tree
through the house,

its needles tracked
through the kitchen,

the living room,
the mess stuck

to the bottom
of shoes and coats,

place the monument
in the middle of us—

even if for a short
time, even if I am

the only one who
will water it.

GOOD STORM

A good thunderstorm
can still knock some sense
into the night, still pull
the wind from dreams
you didn't plan on re-
living, still send a child
from her bed as if it
were a hum
under her skin, still carve
enough space between
her mother and I to make
a house a home, still
find a lake of ageless
water under our covers
where she is still the age
she first found this quiet,
and aren't we just waiting
on the sun to summon
the next shift or thunder
to stop? Whichever
sacrifice comes first.

JORDANS

Copped the new
Jordans today hadn't
planned on any excess
hadn't planned on being
this type of capitalist
even if I was trying to please
my growing child trying to find
some shoes she will age
out of before the year lays
itself to rest the two-hundred-
dollar tag on the Jordans
is not what I need not what
this responsible family man
budgeted for and I don't
really have it but I woke up
as black as my own bed
so maybe I do
have it maybe I want
for nothing until I cross
the street or I drive my car
faster than I should every alley
can be a speed trap
and becoming nothing
is a very real possibility
and maybe I don't care what
I can afford when I'm just hoping
to be here
when the package arrives

HAUNT

After watching too much TV, the little girl
is convinced the house is haunted, every

creaking step or a door finally loosening
its metal clasp to give way to light, it

keeps hidden on the other side a new
specter with a new name. We have a family

of them now, which used to scare her,
but now only amuses her. Made-up stories

about who died first and who must be
fighting depending on what noises

crescendo before bedtime. And this is cute,
I guess, as she says bye to them as we

leave for school in the morning and I
arrive at work later, making enough noise

to barely be noticed and my colleagues often
speak about me as if I were conjured.

IN THE EVENT THEY FIND ME FLOATING

There is never a time when my daughter
doesn't overfeed the fish. I say, *Just a pinch,*

love, and her small fingers always squeeze more
than necessary. The flakes cover the surface

like an oil slick. I try my best to warn her
about the dangers of too much, I warn her

that this is one of the ways we can hurt the fish.
She does not know that I do not know how

to tell if a fish is in pain. I only know how to kill
one. I wish I knew more about what can bend,

I wish I knew how to slow blood without halting.
I never wanted to be God, but I don't know

what else to call that hunger. At dinner,
my daughter moves her food around until

they are countries. I have slightly burnt the chicken
nuggets, so she has relocated them.

For the potatoes I did better. They are eaten
first and then everything and then

there is nothing except what used to be. I try
to remind her to feed the fish when we are eating or

else I'll forget. The fish will starve,
hurting for a while, maybe. I wouldn't know

until I could no longer do anything about it.
My daughter has named the fish—Starry, Beta

& Goldie, though two of them are golden.
She says she can tell who is who, but I don't

know that I believe her. Tonight, I don't
remember if they have been fed. I choose

not to feed them, which I claim as the choice
to not overfeed them. And maybe they have

gone hungry and hungrier still, until they have
become ravenous with want, until the morning

comes and I choose an end to their suffering
if suffering is still an option by then.

WAVES

At the beach where the Atlantic
kisses our feet, my daughter
asks me what the ocean will
bring to shore, like it has
secrets it holds on to. I say
under my breath, *Probably slaves*,
and I know this is me at my
most cynical, a trait my child
shouldn't need to be helped with.
I bury my tongue behind my teeth
like so many shells before
me and remember what lessons
I give without ever offering.
On the ride home, after I have
quieted the bark, an officer
pulls us to the side of the road
and asks me whose car I am driving
my family home in.

THROUGH THE NIGHT

The snow fell and fell on the way back
from New York, the already hardened
pitch of the new day made impenetrable
with a never-ending sheet, and I knew

I could've stayed the night in that city
that was not my city, I knew I could have woken
early with a clear sky and a generous star
loving up the highway but I left anyway.

It wasn't safe or even wise but it was hours
I didn't feel like submitting to, and I guess
it's ironic that I spent so many
years living in death's quarters, taking her

confident hand in my own, pretending to wipe her
kiss from my cheek every morning because I knew
I'd be back, and then one day I didn't know.
What I do know is that once I was a boy who lost

his fear of dying, watched cemeteries get fat
on his friends and then I found you, a home
just outside of the blizzard, finally a sweet
death worth chasing after.

HOMECOMING

I bought the house before we married
     before we conspired to make
          another
a four-bedroom with space for all
     of my ghosts, dear god do you remember
the first time it got cold & neither of us
     had ever heated a house
from scratch before so we shoved aside
the boxes filled   with baubles and Christmases
          before we met, huddling under
my old college comforter, which could've
     been beautiful before
you asked how old   the comforter was and I
pretended
to not hear you, already, with my mouth full
of you, which meant

years & *her*
     & the number I stopped answering
calling
     the rest of   the night
I spent staring at the pattern on the ceiling
     never once confusing them for stars   while
you
acted as if you were too
tired to stare at them with me
besides, you didn't need them and the heat
          had come on

SOMETIMES WE CAN'T DO ANYTHING ABOUT THE BLOOD

Sometimes we can't do anything
        about the blood,
our pediatrician tells us
about our daughter's nosebleeds.
She assures us
it's the dry air   *perfectly*
        natural
not the time I was fifteen and took
a beating for staying
out too late. I don't remember anything
natural about my own blood.
        When I found it, there was a reason, a red hand
that was not my own.

I remember after the belt was applied
        to me
the way I would scare
        birds from the yard

and watch them   become
wings, then feathers   then a single dot
escaping into the sky
          from me.   My daughter gathers
words like   *eventually*
wound   *inherit*   *trial.*

Once I was a disobedient boy
& during my punishment   I was told
          This hurts me as much

           I don't remember
how they slept. I
can recall how the sheets felt like glass
against my striped legs. Our doctor says the blood-
     letting isn't a big
deal, it's natural

& maybe a humidifier will help.
I remind myself a dry home isn't the equivalent
of cold. My elders say
we're too soft.

The doctor asks if we have any questions
but I want to know
where blood comes from, who can conjure
     that spell, and how I'm not an expert
having given so much already?

BACKFIRE

Watching her ride her bike,
a car backfires, a leftover fire-
cracker in August I am no
longer a father outside
of his home, a state
bird flies above
a shattered boy—I am
myself all over again,
trying to find something
that won't splinter, won't
flay like a mother holding
a young death, saying
the noise will soon fall
into fissure. I knew the sound
wasn't the problem
even then, even now
I know what a sudden
stop sounds like—a great halting
can break a neighborhood
until all that is left are
gestures. That isn't
the block I live on now,
I know this, and still I forget
everything built under me
except my name, which
I hold like a long farewell
that has died
once before.

INHERITANCE

Every night my daughter eats a half
measure of her dinner and announces

how full she is, the crust from the pizza still
remains, the corn or peas, broccoli stalks

strategically scattered to the edges of the plate.
I'm not one of those kids that went hungry

or had to bargain with the night to fill myself,
but I remember when my great-uncle

would pretend to eat too and announce he was full,
which was true as he was full of cancer at the time

but no one knew that. He always wanted some
of the cake or pie that Granny was making

and she would say, *But you ain't too full for dessert.*
I watch my daughter plead for the last cookie

before bed and we make threats about eating
all of the dinner first, but I've already washed

the dishes by this point, so the worst we can say
is not tonight. I don't know what it is about

uneaten food that makes wardens of us, but she'll
get the cookie tonight. The last thing I want to posit

is a stay of execution. I remember my uncle would
never actually eat the cake, but would pull

the icing off with his finger, a deep exhale
through his nose, gathering the simplest

of deaths on his tongue. I take the half-eaten

cookie into the kitchen once she's finished,
even if the cookie is not, the icing is gone, probably

still on her tongue as she pulls on her pajamas,
the sweet tailing her to the next world.

MIGHT HAVE TO KILL

the thing, my father says. His voice is a white sheet
    pulled taut over a burial. There is a gopher
    in my backyard. Might be a hedgehog or
    some other terror. Yard freckled with holes
    and shit where the holes are not. There is so
    much yard and now less
    of it belongs to me.

my father, who marched against the war,
    stepped around a uniform by getting a master's
    degree, spends his crop years
    low to the earth, pulling flowers
    from its teeth, wants me to kill the thing.
    It's easier than you think.
    We haven't discussed
    other options. He knows
    I know that nothing will live forever.

I don't remember when I first let mercy have
    its way with me. Maybe after the third fight
    in the first white neighborhood. Maybe after
    the summer they pulled Anthony out
    of the river. Or the morning after
    the fireworks, when my hearing came back,
    but two of our party did not.
    My daughter wants me to kill
    a spider, dangling like a proposal
    from the light. I pretend to be a creature,
    a chaos coming to get her, until she forgets
    the muse hanging from the ceiling. Let me
    be the monster if it excuses me
    of malice. Let something besides me
    survive my recollections.

when we bought the security system, we didn't get
        the motion lights. I wouldn't know what to
        do with an invader if I had my hands
        wrapped around one.
        I wonder now what would the gopher do
        if it knew it were being hunted. I once broke
        curfew and ran from a cruiser to avoid
        its touch. I fell asleep that night hoping
        no one was looking for me, hoping to never
        be seen. Hoping I became a nightingale
        under a green-black sky.

my father says he knows where I can find poison
        cheap. It might take a week to die. To take
        the offering, to die. I say, *But the summer is
        nearly over*, and he knows I am still his son.
        Or at least a boy who looks like him,
        waiting for the sun to finally go down.

CLEAN

Still wet from the bath / the girl has a song /
caught in her skin / she moves side to side /
limbs springing out / like new animals /
stop child, I warm / the lotion and try /
to apply it to a moving / target in and out /
of my reach / hit an elbow then a calf /
the giggles don't stop / and I practice /
aging while trying / not to fire blanket /
the atomic girl / who laughs at everything /
including bedtime / and I finally glisten /
an arm, chest, left / smiling cheek not /
because I have / gotten better but the child /
has slowed with age / and now a playful hand /
is a potential fist / a scarred knuckle /
the one leg will / become less perfect after /
a fall remember when / I wore crutches, Daddy /
not yet am I witness / she grabs the car keys /
my empty-handed / objection, the house empties /
when she leaves / the first time, a collapse /
of myth, I will remember / before I became /
a ghost ship, wasn't always / a bedtime or my /
once-confident / hands glistening, holding /
a brand-new sun /

SHARKS AND MINNOWS

The soccer class wasn't
designed to be all girls
but sometimes you get
lucky and sometimes
your daughter finds herself
surrounded by hard-charging
boys who ignore basic
requests so you test her
with the older class. Here
she looks eight years
old but is not eight years old,
running with the other jubilant
girls, passing with the inside
of her foot, kicking with more
ambition than control
and every so often they play
a game called sharks and minnows
where their coach becomes
an elegant apex predator
and kicks the soccer balls at the girls
as a form of tag. You can
imagine the playful screams,
you can imagine the girls
minnow, lungs darting
away from the would-be fang
of the sea. Once in a while
they invite the adults to be sharks
and I hope I'm the last, I hope
the girls will always run until
their chests are as empty
as a boy's promise. I hope my aim
with a soccer ball is near miss
enough to recognize the pattern.

I hope games will always dress
themselves as games and water
will feel different against their
darting bodies when the game
is not a game but math is simple
so I know this will not be true
even as I keep missing the girls;
sidestep, jump over and around,
taunt and giggle until it takes
all the language from them
and I think for them this is a good
life so far, this is joy and translucent
and because I haven't tagged anyone
with a ball in a while and my role
could not be more clear, I begin
to kick the soccer balls harder.

EXPLAINING RACISM TO MY SEVEN-YEAR-OLD

One weekend my in-laws visited
and they brought their dog Peanut
with them, who lays herself out on every

floor of the house unless there is food
present and then Peanut can't be still,
can't be oblivious to whatever has been

fixed on a plate even if it ain't for
her. Each night when the witching hour
arrives, Peanut begins to bark for no

apparent reason and the girl asks me
if I can see what is scaring her, but my
best guess is everything else that can bark, too.

BRIEFLY WE WERE

On the red-eye flight
the girl wakes up before
she was supposed to, wants
to see what the outside looks

like from way up here
in the heavens. What are
those lights? Buildings.
Cars. People, I say. Every light

is a person, she cuts in. More
like each light is about ten
people, I say. This morning
I am clever and too confident

in my answers. All the dark
spaces—are those people dead?
No. The lie leaps from me.
Probably. She may be right.

Surely there are more people
dead than alive by now. We stare
at the black together on the descent
as I pray none of the lights go out.

THE TRUTH ABOUT FAMILIES

I used to think that every parent
believes their child to be one of one
I know a lot of parents say this but—
and what they are really saying is:
this is the best that my body can produce
and this child is the best future
that my insides have wrought.
Is your galaxy vaster
than mine? I wouldn't argue
that once my wife and I lay in our
too-many-roomed house when the power
failed and the open windows let in
a winter air with not enough noise
so we created a night's sky in our image,
and my mother is still alive, which gives
our daughter more stories than any one
parent of my parents can still breathe into me.
Once I watched a show
where a man's daughter stopped breathing
and his grief crashed two planes together—
maybe we make stars in the sky after it no
longer looks like us, too. Maybe this is
what it means to say your child is like none
other when everyone who was once
someone's child ceases to exist. I wonder
if I could be so vacated by loss
that I would make everyone's best
effort fall from the sky, which I guess
what I'm asking is, would I be so hollow
that I could stand to stare
above me and watch the sun pull
my child away to where I cannot follow?
Or am I simply too old now to believe
in everything that produces light?

DESCENDANT

What I recall about my child's early days
were the deliberate acts of   keeping her alive.
Every spot on her hirsute
crown was a coiled infamy.

Jackal: vampire: klutz: you are
told what   cannot be
done. My daughter had no choice, clung
     to a bumbling assassin. They told
us in parenting class that she would
                         cry because
she is too small to ever fill. What we heard
     as hunger was her literal starvation.
I had not   desired anything with such
throat that I could   remember
     that type of bellow. When we first
brought her crib   into
the bedroom, we had no idea   what
     to do about the night. The night
became the night again and she still
cried. And what was I   if not a totem
          of ill-prepare?   A storm
pulling a lamb to shelter?   We managed
the fever   the next
     year. Sweat   beads on   her
chest,   a forest of splintered child. May
my wife's arms withstand   the shudder
of a giant not yet   told how tall   she will
loom. In the fifth year   she would   not
     be still or   safe or   obey
what we   knew to protect
her. I know some   say the promise is made early
     but this is when   you know, truly,

that someone will mourn
	your death. When		she replaces you
	as the one most apt to harm			her.
I know now that when I say			I would die for my
	daughter		I will gladly play dead			for far too long
until my body is rigor and	forgotten. My joints ablaze
in the			stillness. When I say I would			die
	for my wife		it means I am finally		ok
if we			don't try for		another child.

PLEDGE TO RAISING A BLACK GIRL

You would've thought we set that girl on fire
how she got so cocky, smart as a broken window.

We kept telling people how hard it is to raise a child
who keeps figuring out how to make more trouble

and they just laughed like, wonder where she got
that from? Wasn't much of a question as much

as politely calling us a problem with a solution
barely worth the effort. Do you know how many

classrooms I either dulled my sharp or dulled
my black until I got tired of being the only

kingdom without its own campaign?
How do you know what you have a taste for

if you've been told never to show your teeth?
This time I swaddled her in old blues and new

blues and several choruses I don't plan on
being present for. The elders want us to raise

girls with a song in their heart, but we only respect
the classics if they respected us, which is why

if you ask me how I'm doing, I say still breathing.
If you ask me how I've been, I say less.

Plotting takes a man away from the simple things
like smiling on cue, so I tossed it into a pile

of things she doesn't need. Can't be mad at the talk
back because we did teach her to talk shit

even if she ain't allowed to say that yet.
She still wears all the pink she can claim.

When I say she's in training, I don't mean
to take over the world or just this one world

or that the proper lighting is something
you have to pull from the sky itself.

I mean if there's anything I'm perfect
at, it's still being alive and maybe that's worth

passing on, maybe she doesn't mind reminding
people every day how impossible that is.

INHERITANCE

A car changes lanes so quickly
I forget it is raining, the fatality
this intersection notched last week.
I forget the girl in the back seat,
I forget to signal myself to avoid
a small death or the larger ones.
I forget the Lord long enough
to call them something fit for wreckage.

I can't remember when my uncles came back
from war because I wasn't yet alive. I can't
remember when my uncles came back
from war because they never did. I can't remember
the last time my father cursed without provocation.
I can't remember the last time
my father wasn't provoked.

My yell is a short burst that leaves my throat
a wreckage. The car responds to my whip—
it too forgets the rain to obey me, to save us.
Idiot! I stare out the window, my eyes
hoping to kill a thing it cannot reach. And now
she finally asks, *What's wrong, Daddy?*
But I am fury and I don't want to leave.
I forget the girl in the back seat.

PASSING FOR DAY

This time I'm awake as she,
nimble as mist,
climbs into the bed splitting
the space
between my wife and I separated
by the long
night. It takes
almost no time at all—
the covers retreat
    from my shoulder, then are pulled back
up, not quite to where   it started,
    another rustle of limbs   a knee
    grazes my back,
        tiny fists settle between the valley
of my shoulders   and then it is done.
    Why would I move   now? I dare not
        turn to face her, question
the shelter   she has chosen. A new silence
    is here and I stare out into   the morning
        as the nest behind me hardens
into old sleep. When the soft snore begins
    like a hum,
a subtle prayer laid against   my neck, then I know
    it is safe to rise. I am late
now, sliding one-quarter of myself into
        the dark at a time until I am
indistinguishable among the shapes. Besides,
    building a heaven doesn't mean
you get to stay.

TRESPASS

TURN DOWN FOR NAUGHT

I still fuck with the living,
commuting my soul
from one commitment to the next

burial. I'm not old in the way
that I get bored (I don't sleep
enough. Some days I'm a hostage,

some days I left myself a key). I'm old
in the way I remember when days
were laid flat: my brain was a web

of need. I hunger and acclimate.
Develop a taste for more. I still hunger
in quiet, I still treat the glowing sky

as an excuse for my wild. My body has widened
into more body. My throat will never recover
from the years of fire I called a smile.

My hands are the same size they were
when I was a teenager, but I can't gather
as much to my chest. Barrel and full

and the spot where loves laid their tangles,
where everything was going to be ok,
everything was going to be

ok. Have you ever descended into
a bathtub or an ocean, trying to disprove
a baptism? Have you ever been dying of thirst

to discover that you are the drought?

AFTER THE STORM, IT WAS BUSINESS AS USUAL

The summer of my seventeenth year they shot a boy
in the back in Cincinnati. A week later, they
shot another boy everywhere else. The Panthers
showed up. Carried the casket down the church
steps. My friend's teammate's mother told us,
If a cop tries to pull you over, just drive
all the way home, he ain't bold enough
to shoot you in your front yard.
Henry Louis Gates. Ving Rhames.
I'm not famous enough to almost die at the door
I pay for, though I get mistaken for famous black
men all the time. I get mistaken for still here.
I get mistaken for intent. All endangered look alike.
We had a tree in our front yard. After the lightning,
we had half a tree. The backside of its bloom
sanded down by time. We thought we'd have to
uproot it. What is dead continues to die
until everything else is. It is still there
though, leaves falling from one side of its face.
I am thankful for that half of fall. It is still enough for us
to rake, and bury, and collect during the dry season.
I lied about the lightning, or
at least I don't know
if that's what fell the tree. I wasn't there, but I left
out the part about everyone's garbage cans scattered
far from their homes. I'm not a betting man—
the only thing I can ever put up is myself,
but I would wager the wind brought our tree low.
Invisible and sudden. Like the time a cop appeared
and asked me if I lived at the home I was punching
my garage code into. He could make me
famous with trespass.

HOW TO ASSIMILATE

Before I could make more
white friends the one
I did have came over
after school to watch
Yo! MTV Raps and I went
into the basement only
to emerge later with my
father's shotgun
and of course he went
even more white
because this was supposed
to be a joke, the type of shit
thickheaded boys laugh
at until their sides contract
into spasms.
     I mean, I laughed
even though I knew it wasn't
that funny, even when I had
checked the gun for its emptiness
three times over,
I knew he probably
wouldn't laugh but I was
committed to being the good
son who remembered
my mother collapsing
into a stove after work
and then a couch and then
work again and again
my father retreating below
the house
     and sometimes wouldn't
come up for anything,
even if it was something

he could tear apart
with his teeth. The men at
his job would whittle him
down into a cross until
he believed in it, stringing it
around his own neck,
and when I say
men, I mean white men
    because what other kind
is there? And yes, I know watching
my friend spread himself
in fear is a lot to ask of him, hard
to claim mercy for supplying him
with a parachute
    if I'm the one pushing
        him out of a plane.
I don't say
that to say he was a jerk
to me or that he deserved
it—it means his parents
got him a Starter jacket
for every team he liked
and I never felt right about
not refusing the one
he handed me down,
the one my father said cost
too much and maybe
he wasn't talking about
the jacket anyway.
My friend's parents
accidentally
bought him two of the same,
but the gun, he said that wasn't
cool and he was right
    and I could never really
figure out why I aimed a hollow

threat at my friend except
to say that I probably gave him
something I know so well.
It rubs my back
during slumber,
but his parents
never could afford.

I NEVER GOT OVER TRE GETTING OUT OF DOUGHBOY'S CAR

because *Boyz n the Hood* was a passage.
The camera aims and everybody wants to say
they've seen a dead body until they witness Mrs.

Robinson forget to exclude a name in roll call.
Lord knows we put enough potential into
the ground to make a college of prayers. Please

believe the howls when they've replaced a boy's
greetings. Dear reader, I have worn black and driven
into a night's percussion looking for something

to empty. I have been at the wheel
of my ending where all the wisdom I will hear
last escaped the throats of dead things.

But I have also been a stained
boy forever rubbing
the blood out of my palms until only someone

else's remained on them. I have become soft prey
and given to flight where I have replaced my friends
with silence and asked to be left to wander

into the open claws of a moonless lover. And yes,
my father spent godless nights waiting to yell at his
still-alive boy. He had seen sons get in cars

and transports and cruisers and bar-windowed buses
and never return or at least never call home
but mostly, reader, I guess I am almost

always the car itself carrying the bodies
toward the end of things or being left when my toll
is too high. I can only let death ring

out from me for so long until I
start to look like death myself.
I can only suffer the seal

of my doors closing
so many times, so many last rites
before I refuse to open them again.

MY LYFT DRIVER SAYS YOU SHOULDN'T CALL
YOUR CHILDREN SMART

& I guess I understand what it means to be named
many things but most often after the worst thing
you survived & I guess humility got a lot of
guys laid in college for being mysterious & I
guess there's something to be said for being loved for
the downswing and not just the seduction
of your beveled edge & I guess the only difference
between flowers being thrown at your feet or being
thrown on your grave is what you
are expected to do next.

Here is what I know about my unmaking:
My ACT score was higher than the age
of the smartest kid I grew up with ever made it
to. I once spent a night breaking windows
and the moonlight rinsed through them
because what would I do in college anyway?
I was once a beautiful bouquet of new stalks,
but nobody told us what it takes to bloom.
So many of us were pulled up, root and all.
You don't wait for something to flower if you were
only taught what the ground will take.

INHERITANCE

I am my most imposing during the winter
        when the coats are longer and I
levitate over folks who already think
me taller than I actually am
I trained a stride and cadence into myself
        the arms move like oars through deep
river the river that demands a toll to cross it
I open doors the minimum necessary
flatten my body through the fissure
illusionist among the yokels *watch the large*
man captivate then disappear, watch
the shoulders never dip below sea level
my father used to walk this way
in the ways that my father was once my age
at Thanksgiving or Labor Day
he lumbers into the living room to watch
the game a body slowed from a lifetime
at the forge pounding iron into his missing parts
there's a different molding in the suburbs
where erosion happens away from watchers
I have been told my entirety that I look
like my father and I spent those early years
hiding my hands acting smarter than I
actually was talking my way into fists
when I hear I look like him now I know
it means that the parts I am replacing
have become more obvious
my cheeks a soft and full metal
my crown smooth as a new finish
before the hearing or memory for my tribe
the walk is the first thing to go

the first sign the land has begun to collect
on what was borrowed the feet
then the knees up to the thigh moving
through earth until we have dug
deep enough to cease and lie down

LOOKING OVER MY SHOULDER, SHE
DISCOVERS A LYNCHING

In truth it's not the hanging
that's hard to explain to a seven-
year-old who knows what necessitates
a breaking or a blush
to any place the pain called it
she knows what a hanging does
because she's seen the marks
on my arms older than
her, she's fallen off a bike
and emerged with a new story
running still wet on her legs
she loves superheroes and the way
they punch someone so hard
their eyes close and remain that
way, it's not the hanging
love, we all descend
hoping the plunge ends quickly
it's the easy smiles beneath the falling
of sky, the ornament of an always Christmas,
a picnic made of triumph below a swinging
North Star, yes daughter, you are

right that people celebrating a death
can be a funeral, no I don't think
they are people in the picture,
yes, your friends
from school, from gymnastics,
Girl Scouts, Build-A-Bear, your
teachers and new teachers
look like the not-people too
no, I don't think they will

be there at the drop, at the sudden
dismissal of flight, and I won't
be either, if I pray for anything

it's to know my length of rope
before you, girl, please know
it's hard to tell between
one who will anoint the space
between you and the not-people
that pulled your dad from the car
I would wish you luck
but there are more stories about love
than there are those willing
to die for it, there are fish who
will always have a hole in their cheek
because they were almost
worthy of slaughter, tiny thing,
please remember this picture
and the way eyes can track
their next meal and the smiles
are already decaying, already
an archive of failed endings
before they knew that one
day you could see them

ALMOST HILARIOUS

I remember when we moved
to the white neighborhoods

we must have practiced fire
drills in school so much that we

could navigate the hypothetical smoldering
of halls with calm and docile precision.

We would wind our way through
the turns, obey the teachers to safety

with our eyes closed, but not necessarily
in our sleep because once or several times

an officer placed his finger an inch into my heart
and told me to get my black ass off the field

a block from our new home. I didn't dream
of much else. If his hands were on fire

or if he bellowed my not-name in swirling smoke,
maybe I would've felt at home pooling at his feet.

Which is funny since a lot of black boys
disappeared over the years, some came back

with scars, some never came back
at all, but so few were lost to fire.

BATTLE OF VERSAILLES

The park opened and it was good
and the white folks came and it was
still good and the white folks brought
their dogs and the kids could no longer
run free through the fields and the kids
could no longer play soccer for fear
of stepping in dog shit and we thought
well this is easy they must go the dogs
I mean but the city said yes they should go
so they called a meeting to tell them no longer
will your dogs shit in the park and we thought
well this is easy until it was announced that
a dog park would be built too and we thought
well that's unexpected but we too have
wanted to be given a field and nothing but
options we too have begged for a sanctuary
where the leather is unclamped from our necks
so we thought cool a new dog park would be cool
until we saw that we were the new dog park
except they still called it a park and no one ever
cleans up the dog shit and no one ever forgets
the first time a dog broke free of a leash or an
owner's attention and saw you as a new opportunity

BEFORE: GOOD NEIGHBORS

Dear Neighbors, as I rise before your sun, running
past your homes on my morning penance, knowing
every break in the sidewalk, knowing where you
have hidden dawn for another hour, know
that I no longer come in peace as much as I have
been here for some age, when frost was writing her
name on our cars and mailboxes and before that,
when you left your leaves for the animals to nest
under, I know what it means to fall, not as a single
piece, but a collective scatter, where my remains are
given to wind and crunched underfoot, if you ever
wondered, we always end in the street, before
giving up on being whole, yes, you've seen my
labored breath on the second mile, perhaps your
lights are motion-sensored or you were waiting for
me, your cat no longer flinches from my path, and I
think what it must mean to see something that can
absolutely ruin you and not be compelled to move
from its steps, maybe I am a harmless creature
now, maybe you will never need to call the police
on me again for morning jogs, where I must have
been running from something and I was,
every day is a half-flung benediction, but I jogged
with my daughter, and you remarked she must be two years
older than she actually is, and I knew the sun was
still setting, I knew the night had other designs on
our bodies, you should see the claws I grow before
a hunt, you should see the fur and the teeth and the
way a doe gives me its last breath, this is why I rise
so early to run now, when the crickets are awake
and verbose with song, I hear them because I am
them like any good myth, heard in my most known
form, a renewable fable and never truly seen.

AFTER: GOOD NEIGHBORS

The last white family
    moved from our street
the quiet family who never
    had company who never
threw parties or occupied
    the whole block with other
white people's cars they
    were here before us but not
before the new us sometimes
    you could catch him shirtless
Jesus with no spear cutting
    the front lawn or her still
thin as inheritance trimming
    the growth that would black
out the whole house if she
    ever let it every new moon
I'd see her finishing a jog
    especially after the baby
came about two years
    ahead of our own
and once for the first time
    they came to our door
and asked if we would buy
    some Girl Scout cookies
but I froze and didn't say
    sure come in and didn't
say my daughter is also
    selling cookies this year
and didn't say I noticed
    you never have any yard
signs during the election
    years and didn't ask what
their names were or what
    was the neighborhood

like before we tumbled
	from a more pitiful heaven
but I instead said no thank you
	and good luck because
I have been forged to deal
	with the arrow of starvation
the billy club I have been
	trained to pry the talons
squeezing a bellow from
	my throat but I am still
new at being invisible
	and then suddenly not
I am still learning my hands to be
	as still as an old pond
I am still learning
	to let myself be dug up
again by someone
	anyone for the first time
for the first time there are
	no white people on the street
every silo filled with someone
	who doesn't know if they
belong here or not I suppose
	there's something legend
in all of that I suppose once
	there were neighborhoods
that had white people in each
	home and then they didn't
what became of them where
	did they move to and what does it
mean if they just moved again from
	our street in the dead of night
without so much as a no
	thank you or good luck

SOCIAL EXPERIMENT IN WHICH I AM THE [BEAR]

At the dinner party
I didn't want to attend
because these people
are from work, meaning
[overtime] without pay,
and one woman, newish
person in old money, ring
on her hand that could
lift a family out of the mud, says *[boy]*
I didn't know you were
this funny, I didn't know
you were a troubadour, a silk rousting
my ears and of course I am
paraphrasing because she can't
really talk like me, a [writer] and all
except when she flexes and says
And I heard you write
poetry too, my [worship] you aren't
intimidating
at all, are you?
you're as ursine as they come
and if you think
she didn't really say "ursine,"
then you've never
seen a hunter try to aim
straight with one hand
while they offered
the forest's gifts with the other,
and if you think I didn't know
she thought I was once
a great beast neutered down

to [civility] then
you haven't attended enough
dinner parties, and I wish
I had relevant facts about [bears],
how we are one of the
few mammals that can see
in color, how we can be
vegetarians or carnivorous,
how even a shaved polar
bear is still black, but this time
I just laugh low
and hollow like a stolen growl,
I am already
on my hind legs after all, already
talk with my paws wide
as a preservation, my voice
shakes the leaves even
when I don't plan on it, our lineage
traces back generations, but once
you've assimilated, who's to tell
when you were [captured]?
Who's to argue where the bear ends
and the circus begins?
There's a world between
learning the song of one's claws
against a new throat
and performing tricks
for anyone who bought
a ticket, but I did wash the mud
from my fingernails before
I arrived—I'm still
laughing, by the way, still
hoarding my teeth deeper
within me, I am a [library]
full of the times I yanked
something apart and the times

I went hungry
and the times I let my hair grow
and grow and grow
until I was a snarl of a thing
and I ate everything
the party could offer me,
like I could never
become full

CORIOLIS EFFECT

The email went out to the whole
building, apologizing that they were

replacing the new splash guards
on the urinals. They were doing the opposite

of their intended purpose. My coworker asks
why I am laughing and I stumble through

explaining how splash guards never seemed
necessary, at least not the way I was taught

to hold my body. I hear myself say "taught,"
but I don't know if that is true. Maybe memory

has frozen me. Sometimes, I am
as pristine as a monument. Eventually, I am

explaining the purest techniques and how
I have tamed the curve of the urinal to my

submission, surely sounding like a sniper explaining
the Coriolis effect—my coworker, a cylinder

of amusement, his pale face now autumn and apt
to burst, as he swerves his hips in the most

unflattering reenactment, coughs his contribution:
If my grandfather were alive, he'd be amazed how

soft we've become. I want to join his choir. I know
the song even if my pitch needs work. We are kin

now, in this fabling, but my grandfather, bladder
full of colored water, was arrested for relieving

himself in the company of the wrong gods. I don't say
this, because I am still laughing harder now

for the sake of the pageant. And I should feel
bad, imagining what my grandfather would

say if he could see me, cackling with the jackals
but he got tired and died when I was a boy anyway.

TRESPASS

I catch the lines / of his trunk / he places both hands
upon the fence / the pull / sinew arms / shoulders
rotate propel him / lands soft / the morning wet
grass / I was mowing today / will remember his
footprints / he is a sapling / arms swing low willows
I have no / trees in the backyard / except when he
or another sprout / uproot themselves / when I was
a young trespass / fences were too / much trouble
once we heard / about a kid / west side electrocuted
so fuck (metal) / borders / we listened for dogs
no motion / sensors in the old hood / my father told
me *no more / cutting yards / in the suburbs*
thought he was / trying to assimilate / be loved
then a man / shotgun ready to claim me / I get it
now today I / muster *Come on fam* / to the boy
migrating / the yard I own / he shrugs
barely quickens / his shoulders say / *I know man I*
know but / what are you really / gonna do about it?

INHERITANCE

Along my temple is the vanishing point.
Sniper shot sweet. I tried to trim my beard
before, misjudging the angles that border my lips.
My barber snickered when he saw.
     I don't know why you
do yourself harm, then pay me to fix you. I would
laugh, but he's holding my jaw
like something he lost.

The world looks different when you have aged
out of polite disagreement. I carry my grandfather
to every river I have yet to cross. I have pressed
cocoa butter into my hands until they are no longer
my hands. I don't belong to anything that hasn't
died at least once, so mark me like the promise
you are conflicted about. I have risen from stronger
lies, Homeric reckoning, storm
who swallowed much.

I sat in his chair because I don't always know
myself, where I come together, where I can be
cut. He rotates me like a small planet, checking
me for stubbornness, claiming my new moons.
When I meet my father later, he rubs at the years
of his empty chin, staring at his son, smoke
curling from my new face. Sometimes he snickers,
sometimes he just stares. Sometimes I imagine him
thinking, *I don't know why you.*

VACANTS

We moved in before
the rebound, when the homes
were still cheap. Had our pick
of the vacants. Ghosts canvassed

the neighborhood until we
gentrified the departed. I would
say *our hood* carelessly, we didn't
want for much out loud. *It's so brown*

here, my mother would say.
Everyone had kids, and then so
did we. We fought over who
had the greenest lawn, removed our shirts

during July swelters. Our daughter met
the twins up the block. Then the other black
girls who were a year ahead. The neighbors
would walk their dogs, carrying grocery bags,

stopped to let our atomic girl pet them.
When the fall came again, we saw the couple
across the street rake their leaves, so then
we combed our lawn, and the folks next

to us followed. And God said it was
good. The woman two houses down
argued with a new boyfriend,
and someone new must have called the cops.

The lights stained our windows. I had
forgotten the last time I was threatened.

Naïve boy in my house of straw. I had
forgotten the last time I was called

something I no longer was. Was called
something I never was. Another cruiser
entered the night, and then they took
everyone out of the house. In the spring,

the house was still haunted. The city
planted trees in front of most of the homes.
Ours died because we never watered it.
We didn't know who it really belonged to.

AT FORTY-SIX DEGREES FAHRENHEIT
SOMEBODY BREAKS OUT THE GRILL

Gotta move the cars a little farther
down the driveway, grill brush ready
we never put you away dirty, never
know when we might need you again

meat unwrapped, flattened between
a sinner's palms, sure it's prayer today
fingers spread out like a plantation
but the patties get unequivocal love

hope Gigi ain't left for church yet
who else we trust with the macaroni on
short notice, the kids mix a little till
an adult arrives, you have to have failed

something to get credit for the pastas
and the cornbread usually from scratch
but the temperature just went up and we
didn't have time to prepare, so someone's

auntie gonna do the best they can, might
be her husband (or roommate of eighteen
years and four children) out there working
the grill, too cold to be out under a one-eyed

sun and not be at the grill, but he making love
out there, safest place in a storm is the eye
and you can watch him not flinch, even when
the hawk catch hold of his shirt, trying to pull

him away like the week before when he was
doing some shit he know he had no business doing
he asks for some plates and the new tongs they got
before the summer laid itself down like the barber

we hit every other Tuesday because he stay closed
on Mondays and we were just wearing coats
zipped up to our necks yesterday, I covered
my head with a hoodie, even when we saw

the cruiser doing the rounds because it was cold
enough to risk a malfunctioning body cam over
the elements kind of cold, stomp my feet when I get
in the house even though there's no snow to shake

loose kind of cold, but today the temperature
got all the way up to forty-six degrees
and nobody gonna pull themselves from hell
to our world and call it heaven but what we know

is that today it was warmer than the icy stare
of yesterday and black folks ain't never ask this
country for nothing except the promise that
shit will improve from yesterday, so we feast.

I WILL LOVE YOU MOST WHEN I BARELY REMEMBER ANYTHING

My first two crushes are fifty yards apart
in the same Ohio cemetery. They never knew each other

but now I connect them like a bowstring. I keep
memories like a modeled city, the tallest buildings

erecting themselves between my shoulders. I have
good neighborhoods and blocks that marked me.

I have fires that threaten to burn everything. There
is a phenomenon called "chunking" where

we individualize memories when we're younger
& group them together as we get older.

Time doesn't fly when you are having fun, time
flies when you begin to remember less of it.

I drop my daughter off at school. An officer pulls
me out of my car as the sun goes down. Something

died in between. When aging, the only thing
that becomes agile is time. I now know why

the Babylonians invented days of the week: their worst
day never ending scared them to death.

NAKED WHITE MEN MAKE CONVERSATION WITH ME IN THE GYM LOCKER ROOM

Most of my people have a story
about almost drowning, maybe
because they fell into a body
that did not love them, maybe
because someone pushed them.

The men ask me how I'm doing,
which means, *What has failed
to claim you so far?* I draw a circle
with my eyes on a point behind them.
No, it's not a bull's-eye. No, I've never
shot anything that was still moving.

I don't have a story about drowning.
I have swallowed several floods.
I am nothing
if not terrified of puncture. If I am
to storm, let me not see the break
that lets me fall.

He is still wet as slaughter,
toweling away the shower
as he tastes each word:
*Did you get a good workout
in today? How long
you been at it? I need to be more like you.*

I've never seen my daddy
swim, but Lord knows that man
can take on water. There is a picture
of him in a creek
up to his shins in brownish ripples,

runoff from a river he was told he was
too dark to play in.

Is it shame that makes an automaton
of me? A fast-twitch response?
Does being a quick dresser
make me any less the auction?
Would I ever be so exposed
with my neck within
a snare's reach?

I can see the teeth
of an ocean without
entering its mouth.
I can feel the downpour
of an uncovered man even
when I close my eyes,
even after I have found home
and locked all the doors.

Most of my people have a story
about almost drowning. They
keep the water in their lungs
because someone has to pay
for the trespass.

NIGHTMARE COURT

Two weeks
before Ty dis-
appeared into
the frozen dark
of the East
Side, he held my
friend over
        the railing
of the bridge that
stretched across
I-77 like a pearl
blade capable
of cutting daylight.
He didn't have
an evil laugh
or a love to retreat to
but his hands
were large as
forgiveness
even when
he held my chest
and all its simple
horses away
as my friend
        finally surrendered
his wallet.

My friend cried
harder
when his mom
ignored his yelping
and called the cops
anyway. I guess

what I'm saying is
that I don't miss
Ty and I don't
know what moons
he has left to visit,
but I know what it
feels like to be rid
of the monster
and still fear
the sword
that slayed it.

HE SAYS MY BLOOD PRESSURE IS EXCELLENT
SO DEATH IS WASTED ON ME

I tell my doctor that my knee
makes house-settling noises
when I run and my doctor says,
You're 40, so stop running.
I could have claimed
so many times by now
my knee ain't got enough
bass in its voice to stop me.
I remember. I've been smoke.
A car crash, a boy broken into
several eulogies, and somebody
saw a gun supposedly, but we
always ran before we could
commit anything to nightmare.
A CrossFit class at six means I'll be
driving home at night, full of my
own survival, the quickest way
home, hoping no cop finds me
under such a perfect moon. I'm just
trying to see my girls
again, pray the black of the ending
day can tell when I'm joking—
I didn't really mean that I just want
this day to be over, I was just trying
to squeeze out ten more sit-ups.
The punch line is always
that we're training in case of
the apocalypse or the race war
or any scenario we pretend isn't
already happening. But what does
"apocalypse" really mean? My grandparents

been dead. Zell still
in prison, they killed Bobby over
a turn signal. Teri flinches every
time the beat drops or a man says
her name like a lost city. Curt was
a boy just waiting to go pro and then
he was a white cross along the highway.
By the time I learned the term
"extinction level event," the fields
had already been torched. I can't
skip the last set—I sit for too long
and the future gets bored with me.
You know what they say about sharks?
I'm more concerned with animals
that aren't hunted. If I say I need a new
workout, I'm asking which animal
is the hardest to kill. What beast
is so evolved they just aren't worth
the trouble?

AGING OUT OF SOMEONE ELSE'S DREAM

EVERY BLACK KID OVER 30 HAS A STORY ABOUT PICKING THEIR OWN SWITCH

Even if it was a belt, really. Even if their hood
didn't have trees. Nobody wants to believe
any bullet fired around them wasn't meant
for them if they survive it. If your God is truly

merciful, may you be blessed with every scar.
Suffered the diminished hearing in your left ear from
the summer Wu-Tang took you hostage. You know
the world wants to hollow you out because you

loved someone that was once your age and now
they no longer have an age. You don't know shit
about flowers, but you remember the auntie that
bloomed once a year when the cops would finally

take her husband and his hands to jail for a week.
Elders are the only folks who take cruises because
they took a lifetime to get over crossing that much
water. If you are to keep religion, let the thin trees

with air-whip branches, but nothing tall enough
to swing from, be the totem. Let the man that
blocked your exit remain one man and not
every man that moves into a vacancy on your street.

Everyone has an idea of what their savior's face
looks like but never wonders what the bastard
is holding behind his back. You haven't been right
since your high school teacher told you to stop

showing off in class. Now you get nauseous
when your daughter aces her spelling test.
When you were younger, your father overheard you
talking to your white friends and told you

code-switching will kill you. You remembered
the day he took you
to work with him
and you offered back to him,

you first.

IMPACTED

My father has all of his teeth, even now
after he lost people, lost a childhood
to the sixties, lost blood above his brow,
lost time, memory, recalled what he could.

The smile remains, mostly blood in blood out,
mostly weathered by nightmare or waking,
mostly invisible, mostly in doubt.
Almost whisper, almost ripe for taking.

Full row of survival across the top.
Solid line of succession receding
into himself, unseen, a small Aesop
of still-here gospel, church of weeding.

So much taken, so hammered till softened.
Hard to steal what is hid and forgotten.

Hard to steal what is hid and forgotten
if you don't care enough to lock away
a boy, or man who takes his downtrodden
smiles for granted. I, a plucked-clean bouquet.

When they say permanent, they mean until
you are ready to part or abandon
the practice of staying. I cannot fill
a smile like before, a fractured enchantment.

I acted like I didn't need it, so they took
a molar out of my head and never
replaced it. I am my father now, shook
free of perfect, jackknife to his tether.

My inheritance cracked apart before
I ever cursed the kingdom's successor.

Before I cursed the kingdom's successor
I gave smiles away like paper-cut teases—
to know me was to survive a Cheshire
secret and worship new altarpieces.

Surely I have loved enough in the rain
to pass on something to a child that won't
come apart in someone's hands. What is pain
if not a prayer that never left the throat?

You can bribe a target or child with smiles
as long as it is united and not
a wall of past lives with aisles
of almost and not yet and what you wrought.

Maybe the dentist saw too much of me
in my daughter's mouth. Cutting me out, a new free.

In her mouth, cutting me out. Is a new freedom
the day you recognize gifts then cleave
them from your body? If he is less than his sum,
bury a father before he can leave.

They said our girl's teeth were too impacted.
Better to carve, root, excavate. Blood wells
in any cave where magic was held captive,
bequeathed or lashed into when all fails.

I gave her the teeth and the rot that took
over, the whistle through all her empty,
a new smile that isn't a smile, a look
too close to the one a man once lent me.

And later, which is always, I held her,
wounds closing, looking less like her father.

INHERITANCE

Though they wilt   as well let us
    forget about trees for a moment
the sometimes-tended garden
bushes with modest   thorns
pricked-proven fingers with love for the grasp
and   pretend that blackness were   a shrub

once cured   ready for the earth fresh start little black
    flex like you don't owe   anyone a
language
      or a service   If I knew
the dirt would   hold me like a secret
    I might
    not fear
its embrace   I may not love like my great-
grandfather did or   his great-grand before him
when there seemed
      to be more use
    for it but   I know what it feels like to
leave   something behind
that occupies so much of your body   I mean
all those teachers are in the ground   now
well before
they planned and   I asked my mother if anyone
    in our family opted for cremation

and she never   answered but I knew   from the way

her breath left her throat where   no language
followed that we   probably put our black   in
    the earth because at least
we know   the ground ain't supposed
to be on fire   too.

WILDERNESS

What began as the garden became the overgrowth
of everything; crabgrass, dandelions sprouting
under the swing set, folia pushing
    through the mulch.

I have not trimmed the fence line,
as the days of August have claimed me too,
so the stalks erect themselves like monuments,
the morning's wet dangling high above the ground
until the sun takes what it always takes.

I know the frost will come
eventually, though later each year and I will
no longer collect the clipped lawn or
the blown-off heads

of weeds into brown bags. Like the wild growing
around the fence posts and the porch steps,
I just want to be left—extending
until I topple toward the ground, slow enough
to see it coming until I can bury

myself from where I began
or mercy finds my legs and takes them
from under me.

SACRIFICIAL

I shave my own head now
because I am old in the way
that I have survived enough.
The hum, heat, schism against
my scalp, between my fingers,
in my killing hand. I know
the curve of my ceiling like no
one else could. A neck that no longer
needs to remember to prop the head.
I run my fingers back and feel the shy
needles under my nails. The shaved
country and lands held close
by fire. I trespass against daily.
Which doesn't mean that I don't need
the barbershop. I still miss the good
violence of someone else's blade.
How my head fits cradled
in an artist's grasp, how we both
decided how much of me is worth
keeping and how much
I can afford to give.

MATRIARCH

It is important where
the food came from, but now
the ant carries it in her mouth
and this is a constant. Silently
she moves across a leaf
that has paled from the sun,
the thick vein of the fall
looks like an obstacle, but it is
not. She was built for this, after all,
stronger than she should be.
The world asks so much
from the branch, not the leaf,
to another leaf of another
fallen branch, she has tired
of the ground and finds a tree
to scale. She does not need
to fly. She can make the climb
without the sky deceiving her.
Usually, they are famous in colonies
but this one scavenges alone, hardly
seen unless you know to look.
She disappears
behind some loose bark, somewhere
the tree keeps hidden away
from eyes and wind, maybe
from others. Maybe from the sharp
way a season perishes. The tree is
old, upright in the yard, its branches bare
and incapable of shielding
my mother's home. It has been weeks
since I have been here, but my mother
will claim it as months. She isn't wrong.
I'm late for dinner, but still the first
to arrive.

FENCES

Between the fences grows everything
hard to reach. Full of thorn twisting
through the gaps of the planks, some
pricking the wood while the stem

continues skyward, caught
on other weeds. Dew collects
on the stiffened leaves, translucent
then purple like its host. There are

more of them when unbothered,
burning the soil with more community
until the yard is a harvest
of trespass creeping farther into

the land, where the child does hand-
stands and vaults. This is where
we lose our nerve. A child's palm
drags itself across the natural scythe

of a rock. Shears search out
the necks at a distance, shortening
potential, no ambition of precision
falling onto the grass, trying to spread

its own remains before the pyre,
the slickness of morning now gone,
an evening's breath upon it,
a long-deserved exhale. And now, in its final

hours, the last secret, truant
with discovery. An animal scurries
under the rails from a well-dug-out
and thorned reprieve.

CARBON DATING

In the old neighborhood we skipped
stones across the lake's face,

found smooth or flat volunteers where time
had done its lashing just to release

them across the water. The goal was
to see how far we could travel

without drowning, we all
sunk eventually. We all wake

one morning to a routine, a new
neighborhood, the assault of an alarm

clock, and less water. Is a baptism
any ocean that killed

the last you? What else can the moon
pull away from the shore?

Our fathers showed us the lakes
but never stayed

to watch us throw earth across it.
Time had smoothed them thin, too.

STILL[AIN'T]LIFE

It's not like I cussed in the white family's house
at their dinner table with my parents trying to be

well-mannered ghosts and twisting like fresh fall,
still felt the sun of my mother when I answered

the house's owner, *I'm never gonna cram the night
before a test again* like my father's boss was

an essay I needed to ace or—
either way my mother spent the rest of the dinner

cutting me off in case I said something bestial
again. I know my history, so I know now

that there was a job my father wanted
and a job my father didn't get. I can

assume they were the same the way
I figure that no and nah are the same shit except

for when the locks change. My daughter reads
two grades above her own head and still

says yo to punctuate a lesson like her father,
the boy that pulled his claws out of his pockets

because he was tired of stabbing himself
in the side, and my wife tells our girl

"Ain't" isn't a word and I always want
to complete the downswing and say,

Ain't isn't a word that tried to kill my father,
it was actually "gonna" but every time

I let my clever take the wheel
I remember when my mother jabbed

me under the table for my forked
tongue and I never removed the blade

so all my language became clotted
all my boy a wound when he speaks.

THERE IS ANOTHER

me, I suppose. You may call
it another world, but it's me
         when I'm not
here. Maybe it's the one that didn't
get this far. He still has hair long
and unbound, he is a vessel
of feathers. He never loved
the night's opening, took all
the chances. Maybe he never
married or married endlessly,
taking into himself over and over.

I am exhausted by him. He has
answers for all of my rooms. He never
         made his way to the top
of something large without thinking
himself still large. He never refers
to the dead because they don't die there.
He has several daughters. Not just
the one, scared sometimes, limbs
and jubilant all the time. She doesn't
ask him things he doesn't know.
         Maybe her questions are
easier for his comfort. Maybe he's
made every question a hymnal
she can hum back to him. Or maybe
he lies, and only I can tell the difference.

FIRST, WE DIG

The first thing we did when we moved into
the house was pull up the huge bush in front

of the patio. I wanted to buy a PlayStation,
but my wife wanted to remove the cobwebs first

before any new spiders would nest in our home.
I had never done this before, never removed life

that had been somewhere before me.
The bush's roots were deeper than I imagined and I

asked my wife how necessary this was; my father
said that's a good bush you probably want to keep it

and her father said why would you want to get rid
of it, what is it with you and ripping things

away from their homes? My wife has heard this
before. Heard men issue rattles to things

they can't seem to let go of. She knows what
she wants to grow and what customs take on

fire. We went to work and cut deeper and deeper
into the earth until the bush was free and there

was a hole large enough to swallow light.
The branches and leaves caught me on their way

out. My legs and arms and fingers until I
was pulp, nicked and folded

up on the front lawn. Tangled mess
at my feet. She says, *Now how hard*

was that? I know this isn't really a question
because of course it was hard, I have the markings

to prove it. I search her face for absolution
but she hasn't heard my voice for some time now.

TO THE GARDEN I ABANDONED

Believe me when I say I had the best of intentions
in the backyard with tomatoes and peppers
and other crops that resemble organs—I admit
it is a shiny thought among the tract housing
to plant something found and not of me, nurture
with care and water and light, rake over the body
then devour it. I don't visit my family enough
beyond the city beyond the silks of my house. I
mean to say the first weeks you looked
like a promise and my daughter enjoyed asking
when you would fully arrive, what the budding
flowers on your face meant, and I said something
corny like *Those are its eyes peeking out*
at the world before you gave us the rest of you,
and judging by the month's end you must have
decided we weren't worthy, we had too much gray
in our hair and our eyes were always watering.
I get it, truly. I often wake up staring at the ceiling,
knowing the day isn't worth my rising, knowing
I'm past my best years—my best bloom still sits
in the belly of an other who probably forgot
my name. I can't tell the difference between
a tomato and a pepper before they have matured.
It was a mercy when I finally pulled you out,
my arms deep in your bones until every remnant
of you was ready for the waste and you sat
on the curb until someone hauled you off,
and out of my ambition, I'm saying all that remains
are the weeds I can't seem to get rid of. I have
to assume that is on purpose. I hope that
once someone rips everything useful out of me,
I will still haunt them.

CLIMBING DOWN, I FORGOT WHAT I WAS LOOKING FOR

There are three churches within a mile of our home,
a river that carries the word in every direction.

We attend none of these. I still want a prayer
that only exists between my hands.

A god who wants nothing of me,
head angled to the left

like my father's and declares what is good enough.
Eventually I evaporate on his tongue. I love

a pious house adorned with someone's lord,
someone at their feet or them at someone's feet

or a romantic bloodletting, just not my home,
I suppose, where my knees suffer enough,

my palms pulled toward any light that will have me.

AFTER

During the second hour, with the sun still
stuck in the sky, my father and I hold the cross-

bar of our swing set above us as he tightens
a screw. Then, our arms still extended above

us, he hands the tool to me and I try to make
my side mirror his. We have done this for decades,

the span of me. The swing set began as a lot
of pieces, which he equates with quality, compared

to something already built that can unfold
and crumble on a whim. I once was many

pieces. My father became sharper
with a wrench or switch. He says they don't

build things to stay anymore and I know he is
apologizing for how he left our home, built one

without us. Once my side is tightened, we let go
of the swing set to stand on its own, a bar above

our heads, steady as a firm hand. He reaches out
for the tool, and I know I should call more

often, that I have built a house between
us and filled it with years. We begin to hang

the swings, the plastic horse, the slide, green
and wavy extending its new song into the grass.

He comments on how I've taken care of the yard
and he understands I won't let him die alone.

ACRES

My father's goal is to die
before his   children.
        It is the   only way inheritance
works really. I visit him
on the acres   that he is   holding
        for me. Flowers,
    rusted tractor, a firepit
where things went   and never emerged.

*

My father left   us for the trees—
they do   sing beautifully
    when the wind
                picks up. I understand
I understand. It must be impossible
    to not hear voices out here. It must be
music and mosquito, a truncated existence. They
know   how to find you.

*

My father bought this land
                planning to move
    with my mother out here.   When the house
was finished, the   divorce
        was final. Can you   haunt
a home   you never laid your bones in?
Do ghosts choose   their captivity?

*

My father accumulates everything
          on this land
          except people. Tools, minivans, trees felled
from thunderstorms, one and a half
                    greenhouses, an old
camper (also wrecked by the trees), a weight bench,
     lanterns everywhere. I have never
          stayed
          the night out here. I have no idea
               how dark it gets.

                    *

My father wants to be alive
          to see me settle my family   out here.
          We both know
this will probably   never happen.
     Not in the way
                    he wishes, with all
of his faculties and wits. With my daughter
     running through   the open
world he created.   She is already older
than the art of her he wants   to hang.
     We are all aging out
               of someone else's dream.

                    *

My father's land is dense field
                    and his own voice.
     Were he to mutter a prayer for us
a curse for me, only the land   would know.
          Each visit he reminds   me
what is mine. What I already own. What he   would never
     want me to give away.

142

*

My father talks about how his country
        is becoming less his country. I notice
the shopping
malls are getting closer   and closer
to the land. He cocks
            his head to one side, stares at me
with my eyes
smiles at me with a grin   I have yet
            to master. He wants to believe this
makes the land more livable for his asphalt son. We both
        know it just makes his land
more valuable. We take the heat in
for longer than we need it. I'm just visiting. It is still
        his land until it suddenly isn't.
    On the ride back I decide we will lay him
to rest before
            his granddaughter probably sells it.

LORE

You laugh like everything
is not burning. Make me pinky swear
to sleep better. You say, *It's ok, Daddy*
when I have believed myself
     invisible. Waste not your powers,
love. I don't say this. I say less every day;
I stare mostly. Be nice and say I observe
to the point of obsession. Everyone
     has a science, but yours is a spell. Yes, also
because it's mine too. Your mother
is weaving a forgotten lore. I forget
she is a dream I once wandered through too.

You do the cartwheel when it's gymnastics season.
Until it is all you can do in the living room,
     garage, backyard, half-dry from
the bath. You have your obsessions too.
     Like a candy your grandmother sneaks
to you begging to be pulled
apart. All love has a clumsy wrapper, love. All love is
     sticky to the touch.

What I want to say is that I write about dying
     less than I used to. There is less room
for its ballad, the wailing, the persuasion.
What I want to say is that I have died so
many times. I have emptied
because I didn't trust
     what tried to fill me. I have left
so many behind I feel them like a parachute.
The wind is always angry or maybe I am the wind
or I am always. I wish for much
     and expect less. I still think about dying.

Now it is a guest that has gotten
too comfortable in my home. Ours. I guess I could say
it was once my father, but now my father
is just my father. The night is still a starless void,
        until you can see them, the stars, winking
like a secret, the great-great relative
        someone older is always talking about

and I realize this is how
things don't die. They are loved on by those
        too young to believe in death's
argument. Thank you for allowing me to not die yet.
        Even though I have asked so nicely.

What happens when black bodies are still full of life and ambition? When they refuse to be moved? I have planted a stake in a neighborhood and a future and have decided that nothing will move me so easily. My father, who was born after the dawn of the civil rights era, is still here. I, the boy who can chart the violence against him through the neighborhoods he has lived, am still here. When my father is gone, and when I go, there is another—my daughter—who may have to fight in similar ways. She may have to rebel in similar ways. But she will do it, from her own plot, a governance unto herself.

We aren't going anywhere.

ACKNOWLEDGMENTS

Versions of the poems in this manuscript have appeared in *The Journal*, *BOAAT*, *Columbia Review*, *Bennington Review*, *Waxwing*, *Little Patuxent Review*, *Adroit Journal*, *Rattle*, and other publications.

This book is dedicated to my parents, who endured much and were rewarded little for giving me every opportunity possible. I lived a thousand lives in the years I was under their direct care so that I could live a singularly great one afterward. There is no repayment for that, outside of promising to do that for my own family.

To my wife, who has endured every whimsical idea, every reading that took me away, every evening I spent locked away in silence to craft these poems. I hope to have earned your never-ending patience.

To the writers I am constantly inspired by: to Barbara Fant & Nicole Homer, to Dionne Edwards & Ruth Awad, to Hanif Abdurraqib & Hieu Nguyen, to Franny Choi & Nate Marshall. To countless others who have often been there for guidance or just been there to inspire by continuing to do the work.

To the writers of Columbus, who are relentlessly outstanding and make me even more proud to share a space with.

To Katherine Latshaw, who believed in this book even before I did. To Natasha Simons, who believed in the book enough to give it the best possible home.

To the spaces that created space for me, to the Callaloo Retreat, where these poems began to form, and the Watering Hole, where some of these poems took their first breath.

To those who have supported me, invested in the work, and never let me settle, you are what makes me and this book possible.

Thank you.

11/20